New Year Surprise!

Christopher Cheng   **Di Wu**

CELEBRATING
NATIONAL LIBRARY
OF AUSTRALIA
PUBLISHING
50 YEARS

It's impossible to sleep.
Everyone in our village is busy preparing for the new year Spring Festival.
Father says that this year I will have a special job to do but he hasn't told me what it is.

'It's a surprise,' he says, smiling.

Grandfather nods with a very big grin.

Sister and Mother are spending many hours making dumplings.

'Why so many dumplings?' I ask.
'You can never have too many dumplings,' says Mother. 'Some are for offerings. Some are for visitors but most are for us to eat.'

I love eating dumplings.

'And the hidden coin?'
'What coin?' Mother teases.
'It's here inside one of ALL of these,' giggles Sister, pointing to the plates of dumplings.

I know that if Grandfather finds it he'll give it to me!

And guess what? Tonight we eat those dumplings and Grandfather finds the dumpling with the coin.

'For good fortune,' says Grandfather, as he slips it into my hand.

I whisper to him that it's good fortune he didn't swallow the coin!

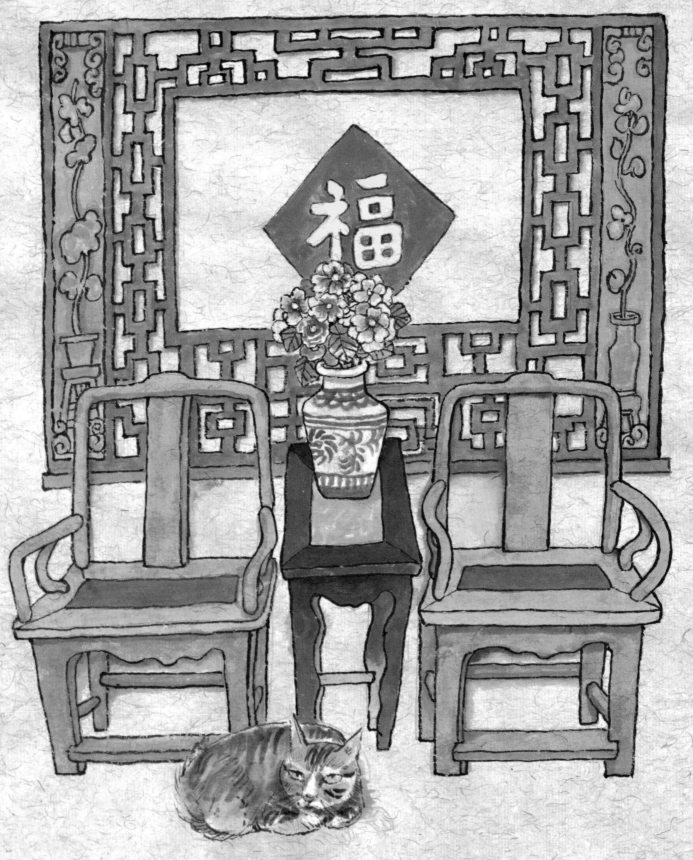

We've been sweeping and cleaning and dusting and shining everything in our house. I can even see my face sparkle in the back of Grandfather's chair.

I open the front door to sweep the dust outside.

Mother yells, 'Ai-ee! Don't you remember Little One? We sweep the dust out the back door. Sweeping it out the front door is bad luck!'

'Gong Xi Fa Cai! Happy New Year, sleepy head!' shouts Sister, ruffling my hair. 'I wonder what you'll do on this special day.'

Father has already pasted the red banners with Spring Festival messages on the front door. He's hung the lanterns too.

So that's not my special job.

Brother's going kite-flying with his friends. Maybe flying his
favourite kite is my special job.

'You can come and watch but you're too young to fly a kite,
Little Brother. You'll get blown away!'

So that's not my special job.

A hawker arrives carrying Spring Festival treats. Before I can even look in his baskets, Father chooses the duck.

So that's not my special job.

I would have chosen the duck too.

When the relatives arrive we give them tea. I smile every time I hear Grandfather telling his stories. Last year I served the tea for the first time.

So that's not my special job.

'Xie xie, Father. Xie xie, Mother.
Thank you, Aunty. Thank you, Uncle.'
They give me red envelopes with lots
of money inside. Then we celebrate
with fireworks. I'm already allowed
to light crackers.

So that's not my special job.

Brother's friends come for the Dragon Dance.

'You're too small,' yells one when he sees me looking at his dragon shirt.
'You can't hold the dragon poles,' whispers Brother, putting on his shirt.

So that's not my special job.

'I could still wear a dragon shirt,' I mumble.

Then Father speaks. Everyone always listens to him.

'I'm carrying the Pearl of Wisdom. And you, Little One, you can carry one too.'

'Together we will lead the Dragon and
he will bring good fortune to our village.'

'That's your special job!'

That night I'm very, very tired. I have no trouble sleeping!

The whole village sleeps too.

On Writing This Book

I was inspired to write this story when I read a book about festivals in China called *Long Established Customs of Chinese Festivals*. This book is in the collections of the National Library of Australia. You can see some of the pictures from this book on these pages.

About the Setting

New Year Surprise! is set in northern China where there are still villages like the one in the story. In the north, it is cold and snowy at the time of the Spring Festival (also called Chinese or Lunar New Year). People wear lots of thick clothing to keep warm and beds are often platforms that are built over small wood-fired furnaces. When needed, these beds become eating places, the quilts piled high nearby.

Many ways of life in northern China remain the same—little boys have haircuts like Little Brother and brooms are made of brush and plates of bamboo. All over China, preparing and serving tea to visitors is done in a particular way, using special teapots, cups, trays and tea strainers.

Dragon dances are a special part of the Spring Festival.

Festivals in China

Festivals have been part of Chinese culture and life for generations and generations. In the past, they marked the passing of the seasons and the growing and harvesting of crops. Today, festivals continue to be a time for families to come together and celebrate. There are sumptuous feasts of exquisite food, like dumplings, noodles, buns and cakes, all prepared just for the occasion. Fireworks light up the skies to scare away evil spirits and people wish each other happiness, good health and prosperity.

One of my favourite festivals is the **Spring Festival**, or Chinese New Year, the most important festival of the year. It is celebrated between the last day of the last month on the Chinese calendar and the 15th day of the first month in the New Year. The Spring Festival finishes with the **Lantern Festival**, usually in February or March, when lanterns of all shapes and sizes are carried or hung in the streets.

Relatives travel from all over China to be with their families to celebrate the year that has gone and to welcome the New Year. People write New Year wishes for good luck on red pieces of paper and paste them to doors or hang them in houses. Occasionally, these pieces of paper are placed upside down. This means that good luck is coming. Young children let off noisy fireworks and receive money in red envelopes, and sometimes gifts and sweets. Spring Festival is a time to wear traditional jackets—red in the past, but in lots of different colours today. Fish, a symbol of good luck, is on the menu of Spring Festival feasts.

'Happy New Year!' people say to each other on New Year's Day. A child is holding firecrackers on a stick.

Dragon boat racing is held in the hot summer. The rowers pull their oars in time with the beats of a drum and a gong.

Dragon and lion dances are always a highlight of the New Year celebrations. They are believed to bring good luck and prosperity and to scare away evil spirits. The dances are energetic and loud and sometimes accompanied by firecrackers.

Kite-flying has been around for a long time in China. There is even an old saying about kites: 'those who fly a kite can have a long life'. Kite-flying is especially popular at the time of the Spring Festival, when the weather is perfect for kites.

Here are some of my other favourite festivals:

The **Qingming Festival**, or Tomb-sweeping Day, commemorates the passing of ancestors. Relatives sweep tombs and bow to pay their respects, before presenting offerings of food and flowers at the graves.

At the **Dragon Boat Festival** there are races in dragon-shaped boats. Teams from different parts of the world travel to China to compete in the races. In Australia, there are many dragon boat teams. Zongzi—sticky rice wrapped in bamboo leaves—is the special food eaten at this festival.

The **Mid-Autumn Festival**, or Moon Festival, is when people give thanks to the bright full moon. Relatives and friends exchange delicious round moon cakes to wish each other a long and happy life.

In the past in China, the number nine was special. So the ninth day of the ninth month is a day of celebration at the **Chongyang Festival**, or Double Ninth Festival. It is a time when relatives and friends gather together to climb a mountain. They also enjoy Chongyang cake and displays of chrysanthemum flowers.

Kite-flying and kite-making competitions are very popular in China. Kites can be any shape.

The moon shines brightly at the time of the Moon Festival. These men are going to share a plate of moon cakes.

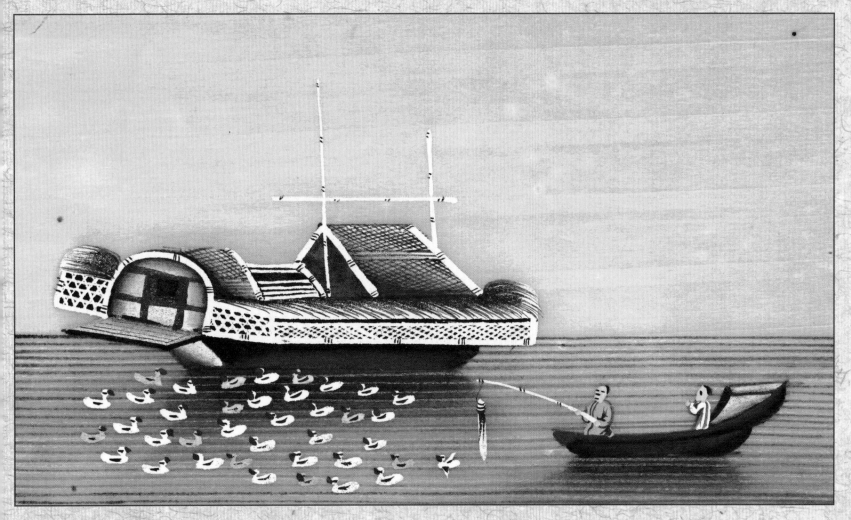

This picture is from *Album of Chinese Sailboats and Other Sailing Craft* (nla.gov.au/nla.cat-vn6485019), held in the Library's Chinese Collection. It is a nineteenth-century painting of a houseboat and a fisherman in southern China.

A Few Words from the Illustrator, Di Wu

Forty-seven years ago I was working as a farmer in north-eastern China. During the Spring Festival, it was snowing everywhere. I decided to go back to Guangzhou in China to paint the pictures for this book. I have tried to depict this festival in a traditional way, by using Chinese brushes and the colours of traditional Chinese painting, as well as by painting on rice paper.

Chinese Collection, National Library of Australia

The National Library of Australia has the most extensive Chinese collection in the country with over 300,000 books in Chinese, 9,000 magazine titles and thousands of other items including newspapers, posters, paintings, photographs, maps, microforms and electronic resources.

The Library has been digitising some out-of-copyright Chinese material and making it freely available online to users anywhere in the world, as well as archiving significant Chinese websites. The Library also subscribes to Chinese ebooks and major Chinese databases, available online to registered Library users.

For more information on the Chinese Collection, visit nla.gov.au/asian/chinese

Published by the National Library of Australia
Canberra ACT 2600

© National Library of Australia 2016, reprinted in paperback 2024
Text © Christopher Cheng
Commissioned illustrations © Di Wu

The National Library of Australia acknowledges Australia's First
Nations Peoples—the First Australians—as the Traditional Owners
and Custodians of the land and gives respect to the Elders—past and
present—and through them to all Australian Aboriginal and Torres
Strait Islander People.

Teachers' notes for New Year Surprise! are available at
nla.gov.au/teachers-notes

A catalogue record for this
book is available from the
National Library of Australia

Publishers: Susan Hall, Lauren Smith
Editors: Susan Hall and Joanna Karmel
Designer: Stan Lamond
Research assistance: Di Ouyang, Xiaoli Li and Irina Chou
Production coordinator: Celia Vaughan
Printed in China by RR Donnelley on FSC®-certified paper

MIX
Paper | Supporting
responsible forestry
FSC® C144853

Find out more about National Library Publishing at
nla.gov.au/national-library-publishing